Rochesternomics

Why, Statistically Speaking, You Should Live in Rochester, NY

Amol Shrikhande

First published by Dog Ear Publishing
4011 Vincennes Rd
Indianapolis, IN 46268
www.dogearpublishing.net

ISBN: 978-1-4575-3517-8

This book is printed on acid-free paper.

Printed in the United States of America

To **Anitha,**

who has tolerated four years of babble about Rochester,

and, even worse, ten years of marriage

And to **Sohan and Sabrina,**

who are too young to realize that their father has issues

CONTENTS

Introduction

Rochester, New York, is perfectly situated to be misunderstood. It is in the same state as the nation's largest and the world's most culturally diverse city. It is sandwiched between Buffalo and Syracuse, two cities that, for several reasons, have attained greater name recognition. Rochester has no teams in the four major American professional sports, nor does it have any universities fully performing at the highest level of college athletics. Rochester's most iconic company, Kodak, suffered an unfortunate decline into bankruptcy. The western New York region is known for copious amounts of snow and, with its location on the eastern edge of the Rust Belt, abandoned factories. Upstate New York in general has become synonymous with agriculture and economic decline. Given the above, a perception has been created that Rochester is a small rural community with relentless snowfall, little culture, minimal diversions, and a faltering economy.

This perception is so strong that prior to moving to Rochester, I was asked the following questions (all with a straight face and perhaps a bit of concern):

1. Why move to a dying area? (The metropolitan area is growing.)

2. Do they have any Indian restaurants there? (Rochester has eleven Indian restaurants and about nine South Asian grocery stores.)

3. Do they have car dealerships? (Maserati and Jaguar are among the options available for those so inclined.)

4. Will you need Spanish there? (As of 2010, 16.4 percent of the city of Rochester described itself as Hispanic or Latino.)

5. How small is it? (It is considered a large metro area by the US Census Bureau.)

6. Is it like Williamson, West Virginia? (Rochester has 70 times the population of Williamson.)

7. Are you ready for the weather? (It is one of the safest weather cities in the country.)

8. Are there any cultural outlets? (Really?!)

Few, if any, metro areas can boast such a wide gap between perception and reality. The books *Moneyball* and *Soccernomics* have shown the advantages of data-driven analysis in baseball and soccer, respectively. Along with *Freakonomics*, these books have shown that data can turn dogma into myth and create unforeseen truth. A similar type of rigor can be applied when assessing America's metropolitan areas. For those able to move past the eye test and popular perception, a significant amount of insight can be gained. Such insight into 11 qualities that describe metropolitan living identifies an unexpected gem on the shores of Lake Ontario: Rochester, New York.

1 Economy

L ocated in both upstate New York and the Rust Belt,
Rochester is often assumed to be on its last breath.
The fact that its traditional big three employers have all
shrunk adds significant fuel to this assumption. Kodak
once employed around 60,000 people locally. After exiting
Chapter 11 bankruptcy, it now employs under 3,000.
Xerox, once headquartered in Rochester, has also shed
thousands of local jobs. Bausch & Lomb, which recently
moved its headquarters to New Jersey, has suffered a very
similar fate. Considering that these three companies
together once employed about 60 percent of the region,
it's easy to see why many had written Rochester's obituary.

Yet one problem exists with the notion of economic
decline in Rochester: it isn't true. When Kodak was at
peak local employment in the 1980s, the local workforce
was about 414,000. Today, the local workforce is approximately 511,000. At Kodak's peak, the Rochester metro
area had about 971,000 people. As of 2012, it was esti-
mated to have about 1,082,000 people. That amounts to
an 11 percent population growth over a time span when
the largest employer shrank by about 95 percent. While
this population growth is far from robust, it is growth,
nonetheless.

Downtown Rochester, which is not exactly known for
its aesthetic attributes, saw an 11.5 percent growth in its res-
idential population between 2000 and 2010. The suburb of

Webster, where much of Xerox's workforce is located, grew 12.4 percent over the same time span. Victor, in nearby Ontario County, saw 43 percent growth over those ten years.

During the recent recession and recovery, Rochester was consistently recognized for weathering the storm very well. At one point in 2012, the Brookings Institution ranked Rochester as having the 3rd best metro economy in the US and the 46th best in the world. In April 2014, the unemployment rate in the Rochester region was 5.5 percent, compared to 6.3 percent nationally and 6.7 percent in New York state. Even *The New York Times*, which has no problems depicting upstate New York as withered and backward, begrudgingly noted on the eve of Kodak's bankruptcy that Rochester has avoided decay.

A widely accepted explanation for Rochester's ongoing success in the face of adversity is its entrepreneurial culture and inescapable creativity. As will be seen later in this book, the slow and steady rate of growth has maintained economic strength (and perhaps increased it via diversification) without compromising the cost of living and commute times.

One may ask whether any of the jobs being created in Rochester are actually desirable. *Fortune*, in partnership with the Great Place to Work Institute, routinely ranks America's Top 100 Companies to Work For. Included in the analysis are an employee Trust Index survey and a Culture Audit that assesses hiring practices, communication, training, recognition programs, and diversity. Any company that is at least five years old and has more than 1,000 US employees is eligible for recognition. Rochester's second largest private sector employer, Wegmans Food Markets, has been ranked for 17 years in a row. Most recently, it was ranked as the 12th best company to work for in the country. (As an aside, in addition to pleasing its employees, Wegmans is apparently also very good to its customers. It has been consistently ranked by *Consumer Reports* as the best grocery store in the country.)

In addition to ranking large workplaces, *Fortune* also ranks the 25 best small workplaces and 25 best medium workplaces. Ranking number nine among small workplaces is Dixon Schwabl, an advertising and marketing agency. Included on the same list at number 18 is Sage Rutty & Company, a financial services and insurance company. Among medium workplaces, ESL Federal Credit Union is ranked number 14. Taken together, Rochester accounts for three of the best 50 small and medium companies to work for, the most of any metro area in the country.

As illustrated above, Rochester's economic resilience up until this point is difficult to question. However, one might pose the question about whether Rochester is well-positioned to continue growing in the future. While this is obviously a difficult question to answer for any metro area, we can look at Rochester's preparation for what is predicted to be a knowledge-based economy. As noted in the next chapter, Rochesterians rank highly in their level of education. Furthermore, per capita analysis suggests that the degrees obtained are remarkably practical. For example, when compared to other regions across the country, the Rochester region ranks first per capita for degrees in physical sciences and mathematics, second for biological and life sciences, third for engineering and engineering-related fields, and sixth for computing and information sciences. Therefore, the logical answer to the posed question would be, yes.

To recap, Rochester's economy is not dying, nor is it merely surviving. Reasonable data suggest that it is healthy and advancing.

2 Education

The school district in the city of Rochester is abysmal. Graduation rates are generally under 50 percent, and certain subgroups don't even come close to that number. The problem is not spending, as New York state had the highest annual per pupil spending of any state as of 2012, at $19,552. While the issue is complex, concentrated poverty is at its root. The solution has been evasive in a big way.

Thankfully, the parts of the Rochester metro area that are not affected by immense poverty are taking the $19,552 per pupil and putting it to excellent use. As outlined in detail in the chapter on taxes, ten Rochester area public high schools are in the top 6.4 percent of all public high schools nationally. Three high schools are in the top 0.7 percent, and two are in the top 0.3 percent. The three top 0.7 percent schools are located in neighborhoods with an unusually affordable median home value of $209,000. No entrance exams, interviews, special talents, or lotteries are required. This is a deal that very few, if any, regions can replicate.

Colleges and universities in Rochester suffer from the same affliction as the entire metro area: lack of brand recognition. While everyone has heard of Boston College, William and Mary, and NYU, the University of Rochester floats under the radar, despite being similarly ranked by *U.S. News & World Report*. In the 2013 federal fiscal year, the University of Rochester was in the top 30 for National Institutes of Health (NIH) funding, a crude marker of research prowess. Its music school, the Eastman School of Music, has at times outranked the famed Juilliard School in New York City.

Rochester Institute of Technology (RIT) is considered a Regional University by *U.S. News & World Report*, based upon its focus on undergraduate and masters programs. In the north region (one of four US regions), RIT was ranked seventh. In the same category, it was ranked fourth for best value. Perhaps more importantly, it was one of thirteen schools recognized nationwide for an excellent co-op program – the same list includes MIT and Cornell. In RIT's case, the co-op program is the fourth oldest and one of the largest in the world. Apparently the university recognizes the novel idea that spending ridiculous amounts on education should at least get you a job. Along the same lines, RIT's student business incubator has been recognized as the best in the country.

The State University of New York (SUNY) at Geneseo seems to garner little attention nationally. Based on SAT/ACT scores, acceptance rates, and high school class rank, SUNY Geneseo is the seventh most competitive public university in the country. This ranking places it ahead of public powerhouses such as the University of North Carolina and the University of Michigan. In 2013, SUNY Geneseo was recognized by *Kiplinger* as the number one "best value" public institution for out-of-state students in the country. For in-state students, it provided the ninth best value.

For those truly seeking value, Monroe Community College (MCC) answers the call. In-state tuition is under $3500 per year, and if desired, the 2-year degree can often be combined with an automatic transfer to another institution to create a 4-year degree. In keeping with Rochester's pattern of understated competence, MCC was ranked by *Washington Monthly* as a top 50 community college among 650 community colleges assessed.

Rochester as a whole has a reputation of being well-educated. Despite the dismal performance of the Rochester City School District, 90.4 percent of the metropolitan area has at least a high school degree, compared to 86.4 percent nationally. Based on 2010 data from the Brookings Metropolitan Policy Program, 33 percent of the metro area has at least a bachelor's degree, ranking it 22nd among the 100 largest metro areas. This ranking places Rochester on par with Philadelphia, Pennsylvania, and Portland, Oregon, and ahead of Dallas, Texas, and Los Angeles, California. While methodology is always questionable, Rochester has shown up on at least two lists of the Top 10 Smartest Cities over the past four years. According to the online brain performance program Lumosity, Rochester is the seventh "brainiest" large metro area in the country.

Whether you are looking to educate your children, obtain a college degree, or simply be around smart people, Rochester hangs with the big boys.

3 Music/Art

Overpaying for real estate and contending with suffocating traffic are often rationalized by having access to cultural opportunities. Most would agree that being able to maintain those opportunities without the other "side effects" would be ideal. While Rochester is by no means New York City or Washington DC, it performs shockingly well on the cultural front. (And as will be seen, the unwanted baggage is kept to a minimum.) What follows highlights some of the exceptional features of the music and art scene – it is not remotely comprehensive.

The Eastman School of Music, part of the University of Rochester, is quietly one of the nation's best music schools. In fact, for whatever it's worth, it has at times been ranked as *the* best music school in the country. Along with a prestigious music school come many benefits to the community, including The Eastman Community Music School and numerous free student concerts.

As would be expected, a community with an elite music school should have an orchestra to match. The Rochester Philharmonic Orchestra (RPO) far outperforms expectations for a region of Rochester's size. First and foremost, the RPO has remained relatively stable financially in an era when large orchestras have declared bankruptcy and smaller orchestras have folded. In 2014, the RPO was one of six orchestras invited to play at Carnegie Hall in New York City. It has repeatedly received the

Award for Adventurous Programming given by the American Society of Composers, Authors and Publishers. This award, which the RPO received most recently in 2012, recognizes a commitment to music written in the past 25 years. The RPO's pops program is conducted by Jeff Tyzik, a highly respected musician and Grammy-winning producer who has had the same role for orchestras in much larger cities such as Seattle, Washington, and Vancouver, British Columbia.

In 2002, Rochester became home to a modest jazz festival that drew about 15,000 spectators. Today, the Xerox Rochester International Jazz Festival is one of the largest in the country. In 2013, the nine-day festival brought over 1200 artists from 18 countries, amounting to over 300 shows, 81 of which were free. About 195,000 spectators packed a total of 19 venues. Artists over the years have included Aretha Franklin, Chris Botti, Norah Jones, Dave Brubeck, Tony Bennett, Jerry Lee Lewis, Al Green, Smokey Robinson, Jeff Beck, Gladys Knight, Herbie Hancock, Elvis Costello, Natalie Cole, Diana Krall, Wynton Marsalis, and Buddy Guy. Given this thirst for jazz, it is not surprising that Rochester can support two jazz radio stations in an era when many cities don't have even one.

For those not particularly into the classical and jazz scenes, there is no reason to fret. A more mainstream sound is well-represented in Rochester. While difficult to quantify statistically, live music abounds. Numerous concert venues dot the region, with both intimate and large venues being commonplace. The following is a small sampling of the concerts that were available in the spring/summer of 2014: The Dave Matthews Band, The Backstreet Boys, Avril Lavigne, Keith Urban, Ben Folds, OneRepublic, Luke Bryan, The Goo Goo Dolls, Weezer, Sheryl Crow, Lady Antebellum, The Black Keys, Cage the Elephant, and Phish. A quick one-hour jaunt to our friendly neighbor Buffalo could have landed you entry to Bruno Mars, Lady Gaga, and Justin Timberlake. If absolutely desperate for a Top 40 fix, a passport and 2.5-hour drive could have gotten you to Toronto to see Katy Perry or Beyonce and Jay Z.

Along with listening to great music, many have the desire to create their own. Rochester's House of Guitars has been recognized as one of the best music stores in the country. *Esquire* magazine voted House of Guitars the best music store on their roadmap of Musical America. The store has also been featured by *The Wall Street Journal* and *People* magazine. Aerosmith, Ozzie Osborne, Peter Gabriel, and Marilyn Manson are just a few of the artists who have shopped there. Metallica, which recorded its first album in Rochester, was also known to frequent the shop.

Rochester's music-centricity was captured in 2012 by *The Atlantic* magazine. Their study used Bureau of Labor Statistics figures to identify the concentration of musicians in metro areas with over one million people. The data was combined with US Bureau of Economic Analysis statistics on the concentration of music and recording industry business establishments. What resulted was a Metro Music Index. Not surprisingly, Nashville, Tennessee, came in at number one, and New York City took the number two spot. Perhaps more surprisingly to some, Rochester took the number nine spot, measuring higher on the index than Austin, Texas. The study's author notes that cities with flourishing music scenes often have underlying creative economic systems that are also supportive of technology and entrepreneurialism. In Rochester's case, it's hard to argue with this commentary (see chapters 1 and 10.)

A final anecdote illustrates Rochester's understated music prowess. During Super Bowl XLVIII, played in New Jersey, the national anthem was performed by Renee Fleming, a Grammy-winning soprano raised in Rochester and educated at the Eastman School of Music. The corresponding sign language was provided by Amber Zion, a graduate of Rochester Institute of Technology's National Institute for the Deaf. Finally, the halftime show featured Bruno Mars, whose keyboardist is Rochesterian John Fossitt.

Other art mediums are also amply represented in Rochester. The Memorial Art Gallery (MAG) exhibits over 5,000 years of art history including works by Monet and Rembrandt. As per its website, it has one of the highest per capita memberships of any art museum in the country. Aside from the MAG, smaller art galleries are abundant throughout the region. The Rochester Contemporary Art Center (RoCo), located very near the Eastman School of Music, has gained recognition for its yearly

6 x 6 exhibit. In 2014, about 6,700 six inch by six inch works by 2,500 artists from over 60 countries were submitted. Each work is available to the public for $20, with the proceeds supporting the center. Art festivals are also plentiful, with the Corn Hill Arts Festival and Clothesline Festival leading the way. The Corn Hill Arts Festival is officially recognized as one of the Top 200 festivals by Sunshine Artist Magazine - this ranking identifies the country's most financially rewarding shows for artists.

The George Eastman House International Museum of Photography and Film is the world's oldest photography museum. Its number and breadth of motion pictures is equal to the Museum of Modern Art in New York City and surpassed only by The Library of Congress and the UCLA Film & Television Archive. The Eastman House was the first photography museum selected for inclusion in the Google Art Project. Given the strong tradition of film in Rochester, it's not surprising that the region hosts five film festivals. Independent movie theaters are very well-supported, and scenes from several movies including "The Amazing Spider-Man 2," "The Thomas Crowne Affair," "The Natural," and "Planes, Trains, and Automobiles" were filmed in the region.

Live theater and dance also prosper in Rochester. Geva Theatre Center has approximately 10,000 season ticket holders, making it the most attended regional theater in New York state outside of Manhattan and one of the top 25 regional theaters in the country for ticket sales. In keeping with Rochester's culture of creativity, the 2014-

2015 season includes three world premiers. Actors such as Kathy Bates, Robert Downey Jr., and Samuel L. Jackson have graced the Geva stage. The Rochester Broadway Theatre League presents touring Broadway shows at the Auditorium Theatre. Must sees such as *The Phantom of the Opera*, *Miss Saigon*, *Les Miserables*, *Wicked*, *Avenue Q*, and *The Book of Mormon* are a few examples of the shows that have been hosted.

In terms of dance, one must start the discussion with Garth Fagan, perhaps best known for his Tony Award as choreographer of Broadway's *The Lion King*. His dance company, Garth Fagan Dance, is based in Rochester but travels the world and is internationally acclaimed. Its local performance home is at the Nazareth College Arts Center, which also hosts the Rochester City Ballet. As an aside, Nazareth has been recognized by *The Princeton Review* as having the 17th best college theater program in the country. Finally, every September, Rochester displays its inclination to all arts with a fringe festival. The Rochester Fringe Festival, a multi-disciplinary visual and performing arts showcase, is now one of the most-attended fringe festivals in the country.

The fertile ground of Rochester has convinced top-level artists to set up shop in town. The famed metal sculptor Albert Paley has called Rochester home for over 40 years. In 2013, Paley was featured on New York City's Park Avenue, with 13 works installed at 13 major intersections. Some of his site-specific works can be seen in cities such as Toronto, Ontario; Philadelphia, Pennsylvania; San Francisco, California; Washington DC; and, of course,

Rochester. Pieces by Paley are found in the permanent collections of many major museums, including the Metropolitan Museum of Art in New York City and the Victoria and Albert Museum in London.

Furniture artist Wendell Castle moved to Rochester in 1961. Often described as the father of the art furniture movement, his public installations can be found in New York City; Chicago, Illinois; Washington DC; and Toronto, Ontario (and Rochester.) His works are part of the permanent collections of museums in Belgium, England, and Norway, as well as domestic establishments such as the Museum of Modern Art in New York City and the Smithsonian Institution and the White House in Washington DC. In 2014, the Smithsonian Craft Show's Visionary Award, given to artists who have "risen to the pinnacle of sculptural arts and design," was shared by Paley and Castle.

If this seems like a lot of art, it is. In 2011, Dun & Bradstreet studied the prevalence of arts-related jobs in America's largest 100 cities. Nationwide, 2.17 percent of jobs were arts-related. In the city of Rochester, 9.45 percent of jobs were arts-related. That was the highest percentage among all 100 cities. In fact, despite being the 98th largest city by population, only 19 cities had more total arts-related jobs.

Clearly, the arts thrive in Rochester. Not only do such outlets exist, but they emerge as some of the finest in the country. To have these opportunities without overpriced real estate and smothering traffic is quite the heist.

4 Leisure

We have seen that the economy in Rochester is surprisingly stable, and at least several employers are treating their employees rather well. Work, however, is just one aspect of life, and time spent not working is generally more enjoyable. A common misconception about metro areas like Rochester is that there is a scarcity of leisure activities. In Rochester's case, the choices are countless and extremely difficult to highlight in a succinct manner. As was the case for the previous chapter, what is mentioned here is merely a brief sampling.

Food and Beverage

South and east of Rochester are 11 linear lakes called the Finger Lakes. In addition to providing striking natural beauty, the Finger Lakes region is home to the largest winemaking region in the eastern United States. With over 100 wineries, the region has established itself as a premier producer of Riesling. According to *Food & Wine* magazine, the Finger Lakes is one of the world's seven best Riesling wine regions. Fox Run Vineyards was named one of the world's Top 100 wineries by *Wine & Spirits* magazine. Not surprisingly, the region has also seen a large increase in the number of microbreweries and distilleries over the past decade. The Finger Lakes Beer Trail, which extends from Rochester to Syracuse, now includes 69 destinations (and counting.) Recognition continues to grow, with *Business Insider* listing the region as number 16 out of "50 Trips You Need To Take In The United States."

Any discussion about food and beverage in Rochester does not last long without the mention of Wegmans. As seen earlier, the Rochester-based company has been consistently ranked as the best grocery store in the country. Given the resemblance to a European open-air market, Wegmans stores are somewhat of a destination in certain states - in Rochester, they are simply the local grocery store. The largest stores contain 70,000 products (compared to an average of around 40,000) with fresh produce, fresh baked goods, specialty cheeses, and international foods being astoundingly abundant. If you're not in the mood to shop and just want to eat, the prepared foods section can satisfy just about any craving.

While Rochester's most famous (or notorious) contribution to the culinary scene is the Garbage Plate, many other options are available. Given the abundance of agriculture in the region, the farm to table movement is in full effect. Ethnic cuisine is also well represented. Admittedly, several ethnic restaurants missed the memo that musty carpet is no longer in style. Fortunately, the food generally outperforms the interior design. In addition to the standard options, more "exotic" selections include Ethiopian, Korean, Puerto Rican, Dominican, Jamaican, German, and Lebanese.

Given Rochester's artistic bent, it is not a surprise to see that independent coffeehouses flourish. In recent years, several Third Wave coffeehouses have opened, allowing Rochesterians to move past the Starbucks phase, if so desired. The Third Wave of coffee has brought sourcing, roasting, and brewing to the next level, with baristas taking their craft very seriously. In recognition of this attention to detail, Rochester's Joe Bean Coffee Roasters was recently named one of the 50 Best Coffee Shops in the country.

Finally, every city that prides itself on alimentary success requires a vibrant farmers market. The Rochester Public Market has served the community since 1827. A typical Saturday can see 300 vendors, 60 percent of which are farmers. A busy day can see 25,000 customers, some of whom may have come merely to enjoy a fresh breakfast sandwich, empanada, or craft beer. In 2010, the public market was voted as America's favorite large farmers market.

Recreation

Between the Finger Lakes and Lake Ontario, the Rochester region contains seven percent of the world's fresh water supply. In the future, this asset may become a coveted resource. In current times, it serves as a large aquatic playground. Boating and fishing are naturally very popular pastimes. As the world's 14th largest lake, Lake Ontario has over 700 miles of shoreline, providing suboptimal yet surprisingly serviceable beaches.

Not all water in the region comes in the form of lakes. As an example, the historic Erie Canal courses through the Rochester region. Once a vital economic corridor, the canal and its adjacent mixed-use trail now provide rather scenic recreational opportunities. Biking, running, rowing, and kayaking are particularly common. Dotting the canal are several vibrant villages that instill suburbia with an uncommon amount of character. Another body of water is the northward-flowing Genesee River, which bisects the city of Rochester on its path toward Lake Ontario. Along the way are three voluminous waterfalls, including High Falls, whose 96-foot drop makes it the largest urban waterfall in the country. If water is not your thing, the Genesee Brewery allows you to drink beer while simply looking at the waterfall.

The Rochester area is home to over 12,000 acres of parkland. The famed landscape architect Frederick Law Olmsted, perhaps best known for co-designing Central Park in New York City, graced the city of Rochester with four beautiful parks. Highland Park is best known for its lilacs, while Maplewood Park houses a nationally accredited rose garden. Genesee Valley Park is a popular gathering spot for sports enthusiasts, and Seneca Park's big draw is its zoo.

Letchworth State Park, located 35 miles southwest of Rochester, provides an additional 14,350 acres with about 66 miles of hiking trails. Known as the "Grand Canyon of the East," the 17 mile long park contains a striking gorge formed by the Genesee River. The resultant cliffs can reach as high as 600 feet. Letchworth affords access to a vast array of outdoor activities. In fact, the park can be reached from Rochester by bicycle using the Genesee Valley Greenway, a scenic mixed-use trail.

Finding a place to golf in Rochester is almost too easy. To be precise, 62 resort, semi-private, and public golf courses are within a 45-mile radius of the center of Rochester. *Golf Magazine* and the National Golf Foundation have recognized Rochester as the 10th Best Golf City in America, in particular highlighting the affordability. To quote: "Baby, it's cold up here, but by Memorial Day you can play more gorgeous golf for less than in any other big American city." *Golf Digest* has ranked the courses at Oak Hill Country Club and Country Club of Rochester among the Top 100 greatest in the country.

Downhill skiing is also easily accessible. About 35 miles from downtown Rochester, Bristol Mountain offers in the vicinity of 33 trails at all difficulty levels. With a vertical rise of 1,200 feet, the resort claims to have the highest vertical between the Adirondacks and the Rocky Mountains. Swain Resort is about 60 miles from downtown, and Holiday Valley Resort in Ellicottville, New York, can be reached in just over 100 miles. Holiday Valley was ranked by *SKI Magazine* as the fifth best ski resort in eastern North America. For true novices, especially children, learn to ski programs are available within 15 miles of downtown. Cross-country skiing can be done essentially anywhere in the region.

Not surprisingly, *Places Rated Almanac* ranked Rochester 7th among 225 metro areas for recreational amenities. Given this immense number of recreational opportunities, it would follow that Rochester led the country in Olympic athletes per capita for the 2012 Summer Olympics (1.7 per 100,000 people.) Local athletes won a total of nine medals, which would have tied Rochester for 24th place on the medal count *by country*.

Museums, Zoo, Amusement Park, Festivals, Shopping, etc.

The Strong National Museum of Play is consistently recognized as one of the best children's museums in the country. *Forbes* deemed it to be one of the 12 best in the nation, while Parents.com included the museum in its top 10. The Rochester Museum & Science Center, along with its Strasenburgh Planetarium, provides another popular outlet for area children. The Seneca Park Zoo, located in Seneca Park, is a very manageable facility that is also perfect for little ones. Open since 1894, it remains the only home of African elephants in New York state. Seabreeze Amusement Park, adjacent to Lake Ontario, is the nation's 4th oldest and the world's 12th oldest amusement park. Located perhaps seven miles from downtown, the park provides spectacular views, along with relatively affordable diversions. This constellation of assets contributes to Rochester's reputation of being very family-friendly. Within the past four years, both *Forbes* and *Kiplinger* have ranked Rochester as one of the five best metropolitan areas in which to raise a family.

From May to October, Rochester is home to an immense number of outdoor festivals – at latest count, over 140 such events occur, with many lasting multiple days. Aside from several popular festivals mentioned in the previous chapter, other options include the Park Avenue Summer Arts Festival (which draws a quarter million visitors), the Lilac Festival (which draws a half million visitors over 10 days), the Greentopia Festival (a celebration of the green movement), and the Puerto Rican Festival.

An occasional complaint that is overheard about Rochester is the lack of high-end shopping. Apparently, the need to spend ludicrous amounts of money on things like shirts, purses, and socks is critical to some people. For better or worse, Rochester seems to be improving in this regard. Recent additions to the shopping scene include Von Maur (the Midwest version of Nordstrom), Brooks Brothers, and Michael Kors. The Rochester area has three malls, Premium Outlets with about 100 stores, and an immense number of local boutiques. It is safe to say that plenty of overpriced items are readily available.

Spectator Sports

It takes a true sports fan to embrace the minor leagues, so to say that Rochester is a great sports town is an overstatement. Having said that, Rochester does the minor leagues very well. The Rochester Red Wings, currently the Triple A affiliate of the Minnesota Twins, have been playing baseball since the 19th century. Notable players have included Cal Ripken Jr., Bob Gibson, and Stan Musial. A family of four can park and enjoy a game for as little as $34 - not bad, considering the average price of one ticket at Yankee Stadium is in the $60 range. The Rochester Americans are the AHL affiliate of the NHL's Buffalo Sabres. Despite a brief separation, this storybook hockey marriage has united western New Yorkers for over three decades. The Rochester Rhinos soccer team remains the only non-Major League Soccer (MLS) team to win the US Open Cup since the MLS began play. In 2013, *Street & Smith's Sports Business Journal* ranked Rochester as the second best minor league market in the country.

Rochester does have some athletes playing at the highest level in their respective sports. The Western New York Flash competes in the National Women's Soccer League and plays all its home games in Rochester. Abby Wambach, who holds the record for both men and women for most international goals, plays for the Flash. (Wambach also happens to be a Rochester native.) Rochester also has teams in Major League Lacrosse and the National Lacrosse League. (Please note that watching lacrosse is not a reason to move here.)

Truly big time sports do grace the Rochester land-scape from time to time. Oak Hill Country Club's famed golf course has hosted The Ryder Cup, the US Open, and the PGA championship. Rochester has also hosted the LPGA championship for several years in a row, although this relationship is due to end after 2014. The Finger Lakes village of Watkins Glen is an annual stop for the NASCAR Sprint Cup Series. The Buffalo Bills training camp is held in the Rochester suburb of Pittsford. Speaking of the Bills, their home stadium in Orchard Park, New York, is about an hour drive from Rochester. The First Niagara Center, home to the Buffalo Sabres, can be reached in about the same amount of time. Finally, proximity to Syracuse provides easy access to big-time college football and basketball.

Music/Art

For those who are musically and artistically inclined, please refer to the previous chapter.

All said, Rochester has the leisure offerings of a much larger metro area. As we are about to see, the ability to have such a fulfilling life does not mandate absurd housing costs.

5 Cost of Living

In an ideal world, income should exceed expenses. When this standard is met, we are able to save money, buy certain luxury items, and generally relax. Medical literature has noted an association between financial stress and the metabolic syndrome; i.e., higher levels of financial stress are associated with a risk for diabetes, obesity, and high blood triglycerides. Unfortunately, most people cannot increase income at will. In fact, from 2000-2011, the median income for working-age households actually dropped by 12.4 percent. To complicate matters, gas prices more than doubled over that time span. And at last check, college tuition is not getting cheaper. On the bright side, some degree of modifiability does exist, with a large chunk of wiggle room coming from housing costs.

Rochester is a stand out in terms of affordable housing. According to Zillow.com, the current home value index across the country is $176,500. In the Rochester region, the same index is $125,100. In other words, there is almost a 30 percent discount on housing in Rochester compared to the national average. In 2011, Zillow.com, in conjunction with *Forbes*, sought to identify ideal locations to buy a home. The 125 largest metro areas were studied with four main measures: affordability (home price to income ratio), unemployment, foreclosure rates, and year-over-year housing price trends. Rochester was identified as the best place to purchase a home. Given the disproportionate influence of housing costs on cost of living, it is not surprising that *Forbes* also ranked Rochester as the 4th most affordable metro area in the country. More recently, the 10th Annual Demographia International Housing Affordability Survey of 2014 identified Rochester as having the 3rd most affordable housing of 52 major US markets studied. Interestingly, of 360 markets in nine countries, Rochester had the 36th most affordable housing.

As has been seen previously, affordable living in Rochester does not come at the expense of top-level education. Nor does it necessitate lost cultural and recreational opportunities. This unique combination of cost control and cultural fulfillment was captured in 2011 by MSN Real Estate. The MSN analysis sought to identify livable bargain markets by first establishing the most affordable of the nation's 100 largest metro areas. Livability was then defined by low unemployment, short commute times, and ample cultural and recreational diversions. Rochester was identified as the most livable bargain market in the country.

One other potential component of cost of living warrants mention. Healthcare in Rochester has been recognized for many years as being particularly efficient. In the early 1990s, as Bill and Hillary Clinton unsuccessfully pushed for healthcare reform, they repeatedly cited Rochester as a model to follow. In 2013, the Institute of Medicine studied Medicare spending in 306 different US regions. Rochester's per member per month Medicare spending was $174 lower than the monthly national mean.

This finding gave Rochester the lowest Medicare spending rate in the nation. Aggressive regional planning that avoids unnecessary hospital expansions and technology upgrades is at least partially responsible for this cost-containment. Such unnecessary measures are ultimately paid for by insurers, causing them to drive up premiums in order to maintain profitability. Not surprisingly, when New York state rolled out its new health insurance marketplace as part of the Affordable Care Act, Rochester had the lowest premiums. Commercial insurance costs in Rochester have been noted to be 30 percent below the national average.

While income is difficult to increase on demand, cost of living can fortunately be modified. In this regard, Rochester provides an ideal mix of affordable housing and affordable healthcare without compromising the intangibles that augment quality of life.

6 Commute Times

The addition of ten minutes to a round-trip commute is relatively negligible. That is, unless the addition occurs 240 times per year, accounting for 2400 minutes. Looked at another way, adding five minutes to a one-way commute can cost you 40 hours over the course of a year. Ten minutes one way can cost 80 hours, and 30 minutes one way can cost 240 hours, i.e., 10 full days. When people take pride in their fast pace of life, they may actually be referring to the fact that their year has been shortened by many days, leaving less time to accomplish life's goals.

Not only do short commutes save time, they may perhaps save lives. A study published in 2012 studied the cardiovascular and metabolic risks of commuting in 4297 adults in Texas. Given that commuting is a sedentary behavior, the results are not surprising. Longer commutes were associated with lower physical activity and lower cardiorespiratory fitness. Longer commutes were also associated with a higher body mass index, waist circumference, blood pressure, and metabolic score (which essentially looked at the risk of diabetes and high cholesterol.) Finally, the authors linked long commutes to depression, anxiety, and social isolation. This study is just one of many linking long commutes to maladies such as obesity, neck pain, loneliness, and insomnia. Commuting is thus a double whammy, adding unhealthy behavior while subtracting time left to compensate.

More recently, a Swedish study evaluated the relationship between commuting and divorce. Couples in which one partner commuted over 45 minutes were 40 percent more likely to divorce. While the data does not appear to be corrected for potential confounders, it does raise yet another possible complication of commuting.

Fortunately, Rochester is well-recognized for a rather painless trip to the office and back. In 2011, Kiplinger sought to identify the best city for commuters. In order to qualify, the metro area had to have at least one million people as well as a low congestion cost (a measure of wasted time and fuel as calculated by the Texas Transportation Institute). Included in the analysis were average commute times, local gas prices, yearly delays per commuter, and public transit use. Rochester was identified as the best city for commuters. Making this achievement all the more remarkable is the fact that New York state is not known for cheap gas.

The average commute in Rochester was 18.7 minutes compared to 25 minutes nationally, a saving of over 50 hours per year. Yearly delays per commuter were 12 hours in Rochester compared to 34 hours nationally. Finally, the yearly congestion cost per commuter in Rochester was $273 compared to $808 nationally. Rochester's nearest competitor had a yearly congestion cost per commuter of $388. Thus, not only are Rochester's commute times short, but they are traffic-free.

Given all the time and money saved, it is not surprising that Rochester has the second highest rate of volunteerism among the 51 largest metro areas. Nor is it surprising that CNN Money identified Rochester as the second least stressed out large metro area in the country.

In short, the average commuting Rochesterian saves over two full days compared to the average commuting American. As an added bonus, there is a congestion cost savings of $535 per year. While good health and a good marriage are by no means guaranteed, at least the chances are increased.

7 Weather

Rochester is synonymous with snow. Examination of snowfall statistics in America's metro areas shows that this label is well-deserved. Rochester averages about 100 inches of snowfall per year, making it the third snowiest city with a population over 100,000. Media reports tend to focus upon large storms, massive snow piles, and people trying to extricate cars from snow banks. Snow and frigid cold are often lumped together as partners. Visions of Siberia and northern Canada are evoked.

A closer look at some data, however, points to a much more mundane existence. Rochester receives at least 0.1 inch of snow an average of 65.9 days per year. Given that total annual snowfall is about 100 inches, average accumulation per snow-event is just over 1.5 inches. While this accumulation may be newsworthy in Atlanta or Dallas, it is hardly notable in the northeast. Looked at in another way, Rochester gets over 10 inches of snow in a storm less than once per year. Much is made of a long winter beginning in November and ending in March. In reality, November on average has 0.5 days that receive three or more inches of snow – in other words, an average of two Novembers must pass to have one day with three inches of snow. While March can be a bit snowier, one still has to wait for two Marches to have three days with three inches of snow. Given that 65.9 days have measurable snow, that leaves 299.1 days (82 percent) with no snow.

As mentioned above, snow and bitter cold are often thought to go hand in hand. While a correlation clearly exists, it is far from perfect. A close look actually points to the relative "warmth" of Rochester. For example, despite having a very similar latitude to Madison, Wisconsin (which receives about half the yearly snowfall), Rochester's average December to February temperature is 5.4 degrees warmer. Similarly, relatively "southern" cities such as Omaha and Lincoln in Nebraska actually boast colder winters than Rochester.

It is clear that the average winter in Rochester may not be as dramatic as advertised. That said, there is clearly a winter, and some people may need more convincing. Perhaps there are actually benefits to a winter. Thinking along these lines, the Weather Channel identifies the following weather-related events as potentially fatal: flooding, lightning, tornadoes, tropical cyclones, snow/ice storms, extreme heat, and extreme cold. Among them, direct deaths attributable to snow/ice and cold are relatively rare. In 2012, an analysis of cities in which these weather phenomena were minimized identified Rochester as one of the two safest weather cities in the northeast (and one of eight safe weather cities nationally.) To paraphrase the study, if you can tolerate winter, you may live in a safer weather city.

One limitation of the above study was that deaths from traffic accidents due to winter weather were not included. Perhaps this exclusion might nullify the safety of Rochester. Fortunately, the local newspaper *The Democrat and Chronicle* studied traffic fatalities in Monroe County, New York, from 2003-2012. There were 257 crash fatalities on clear weather days and 21 on wintry weather days. If we assume that wintry weather occurs on 65.9 days per year (the days with measurable snow), that amounts to 659 days over 10 years. Twenty-one fatalities over 659 days amounts to 0.03 fatalities per wintry day. Similar logic shows that 0.09 fatalities occurred per clear weather day. As such, a catastrophic driving outcome is three times more likely in clear weather.

If none of the above sounds appealing, perhaps insight into the summer might. Spending a summer in Seattle, Washington; Portland, Oregon; San Francisco, California; San Jose, California; or San Diego, California, is widely viewed as desirable. Rochester, with a mean daily temperature of 69 degrees from June-August, is in this select group of large cities with mean June-August temperatures in the sixties.

Taken together, Rochester receives frequent but rather unimpressive snow accumulation events and is warmer than would be expected by latitude alone. The often cited concern of winter driving may be a nuisance but is actually safer than clear weather driving on the same roads. Natural disasters are rare, and summers are remarkably pleasant. The weather in Rochester, usually viewed as a liability, may perhaps be (gasp) an asset.

8 Taxes

N ew York state is not known as a tax-friendly state. In 2010, the Tax Foundation identified New York as having the third highest state and local tax burden per capita in the country. State and local taxes accounted for 12.8 percent of New York state income, the highest percentage in the country. These types of figures have given New York the reputation of being unfriendly to business. To be fair, the taxes inherently are not damaging businesses. Intense state-to-state competition simply allows businesses to shop around and find the cheapest tax deal. New York state has struggled in this game. While New York City can perhaps overcome this issue just by being New York City, reputationally challenged upstate cities such as Rochester are not as lucky. Rochester has had to resort to impressive tax incentive packages that level the playing field but carry their own controversies.

Fortunately, our complex society generally allows for another side to every story. While taxes may carry a downside, simple research identifies (gasp again) a potential upside. Close analysis of the tax scene in Rochester shows all the usual culprits such as income tax, sales tax, gas tax, etc. There is, however, one clear outlier that puts Rochester on the map: property tax. Monroe County, New York, has at times earned the distinction of having the highest property taxes relative to property value in the entire nation. On average, residents in Monroe County pay 2.89 percent of their home value in property tax. About 60 percent of this tax goes to supporting the local school district. So perhaps, if the school performance is also exceptional, this tax can be rationalized.

(Disclaimer: the underperforming Rochester City School District suffers from immensely concentrated poverty, and the following data looks at the metro area as a whole.) Every year, *US News & World Report* ranks America's best public high schools, taking into account state assessments and college preparedness. Most recently, 31,242 public high schools (including magnet and charter schools) were assessed, with sufficient enrollment and data being available on 19,411. Two-thousand and nineteen schools were ranked, accounting for the top 6.4 percent. The Rochester area had 10 schools in the top 6.4 percent, or about 1 per 110,000 people. Nationally, a top 6.4 per-cent school was present at a rate of 1 per 155,522 people. Therefore, you are 41 percent more likely than national average to land in a top school district in the Rochester area. What makes this statistic all the more impressive is that all 10 Rochester area schools were plain old regular town schools. None require interviews, special talents, entrance exams, lotteries, or transportation. You can just show up in town and go where the yellow bus takes you.

One town in particular highlights another important point. Pittsford, New York, an upscale suburb of Rochester, has two high schools that are ranked in the top 100 in the nation. One might expect that this elite level of performance comes at an unaffordable cost. Fortunately,

Rochester, in addition to being known for high property taxes, is also known for very affordable property (see Chapter 5.) The median home value in Pittsford is about $254,000. While the resultant property tax bill is by no means negligible, it is not as outrageous as expected and is softened much further by one of the best school districts in the country. And again, you just show up and get on the bus. Other similar school districts in the top 100 might include Bethesda, Maryland, with a median home value of $802,600, and Rye, New York, near New York City, with a median home value of $1.5 million.

Most agree that education is a good thing. The following tax "upside" may be somewhat more controversial: healthcare. The chunk of property tax that is not directed to schools is directed to other local entities – or, as the local entities would argue, mandates coming down from the state. In the case of New York, one such mandate is Medicaid. In 2012, New York had the largest Medicaid spending of any state in the country, at over $53 billion. Granted New York has a large population, but more populated Texas spent only $28 billion. New York, therefore, spent 2.5 times per capita more than Texas. Not surprisingly, Texas is America's most uninsured state, while New York is among the 11 most insured. As of 2011, only nine percent of Rochester was uninsured, landing it on a list of the 25 most insured American cities. The idea that people deserve health care seems to be very touchy, so this finding won't be labeled as good…just potentially positive.

In summary, high taxes in Rochester have likely contributed to slow job growth, since businesses have cities in 49 other states from which to choose. High taxes have also probably helped create exceptional public schools (despite very modest housing prices) and near universal health care.

9 Transportation

In typical American fashion, the automobile dominates the Rochester transportation scene. Fortunately, as seen in Chapter 6, Rochester pulls this off better than any other large metro area. The yearly congestion cost per commuter is $273, compared to $808 nationally. Intertwined with this statistic is the fact that yearly fuel wasted per commuter reaches just 11 gallons, compared to 28 gallons nationally. Despite a relatively blissful driving experience, the 2010 American Community Survey found the city of Rochester to have one of the 50 highest rates of public transit commuting to work among cities with over 100,000 inhabitants.

In September 2008, the Rochester Genesee Regional Transportation Authority (RGRTA) was featured in *The New York Times* as a model (albeit quite small) for larger cities. At the time of the article, the debt-free RGRTA was actually *lowering* its one-way fare from $1.25 to $1.00. More recently, local ridership continues to increase, and a new $50 million downtown transit center is due to open in late 2014. The $1.00 fare, among the lowest nationally, apparently continues to be sufficient, as it has not changed.

In terms of other transportation alternatives, such as bicycling and walking, Rochester cannot compare to New York City. Again, however, Rochester holds its own. In *Bicycling* magazine's feature of America's Top 50 Best Bike Cities, Rochester sneaked in comfortably at number 50.

For those combining alternative means of transportation, every RGRTA bus has a bike rack. As far as walkability, Rochester also fares rather well. It has been known at times to appear on lists of the most walkable cities, once being ranked as the 17th most walkable city in the country. Recent US Census Bureau data showed that 6.2 percent of residents in the city of Rochester walked to work, ranking it as 15th among cities with over 200,000 people (just behind Minneapolis, Minnesota, and Chicago, Illinois.)

Similar to commuting within Rochester, getting in and out of Rochester is relatively painless. Admittedly, the Greater Rochester International Airport uses the term "international" rather loosely – a quick flight over Lake Ontario to Toronto apparently earns this label. On the other hand, major airports in American cities such as New York City; Philadelphia, Pennsylvania; Washington DC; Atlanta, Georgia; and Chicago, Illinois, are easily accessible. The average ticket price out of the airport is 6 percent below national average, giving it the 31st lowest airfare of the Top 100 airports. Wi-Fi is free, and shuttle parking is a bargain at around $6.25 per night. For those who don't need a shuttle and carry cash, parking can be found for $3 per night.

Train travel to and from Rochester exemplifies the tried and true American tradition of "slow speed rail." The local "temporary" Amtrak station, in use since 1978, is an embarrassment. Despite these flaws, the train does show up and provides decent access to New York City; Toronto, Ontario; and Chicago, Illinois. Mercifully, the train station is due for a $26.5 million dollar upgrade. Talk of high speed rail is rampant, but please do not expect anything before the turn of the century. Bus travel is also readily available.

Transportationally speaking, Rochester does quite well. Driving is actually pleasant, and public transportation is surprisingly well-developed. Pedestrians and cyclists are well-represented. Air, train, and bus travel, while not particularly spectacular, are more than sufficient.

10 Ingenuity

As noted in Chapter 3, there is no dearth of creativity in Rochester. The culture of originality that has allowed the arts to thrive has also translated into a remarkably inventive business community. Dating back well over a century, Rochester has been notably productive in this regard. Western Union took the lead in telegrams. Kodak brought photography into the household. Xerox made the copier mainstream. Bausch & Lomb took lens manufacturing to a higher level. Even one of our favorite condiments, mustard, hit the big time thanks to Rochester's Robert and George French (think French's.) More recently, the Food Channel called Wegmans the "Grocery Store Chain That Most Changed the Way We Shop."

Despite the downsizing and/or relocation of some of Rochester's iconic companies, innovation remains part of the community fabric. In 2013, The Brookings Institution released a report on patent production in 360 metro areas. From 2007-2011, Rochester had the 13th most patents per million residents (with the largest subcategory of its patents coming in optics.) Rochester frequently finds itself on lists of the most innovative American cities. In 2010, *Forbes* studied the 100 largest metro areas in terms of patents per capita, venture capital investment per capita, and ratios of high tech, science, and "creative" jobs. Based upon this methodology, Rochester was found to be the 14th most innovative city in the country. Going hand in hand with innovation is research productivity. In 2013, an article in *Scientific Reports* identified key cities worldwide in terms of the production and consumption of knowledge in physics. Rochester ended up 18th among this group of the world's leading centers of physics. This ranking put Rochester in the company of cities like London, Paris, and Tokyo.

Being recognized for ingenuity is more than just a source of pride. Ingenuity may be closely tied to economic vitality. As noted in Chapter 1, Rochester has seen overall job growth despite seeing its largest employer shrink by 95 percent. Furthermore, ingenuity seems to associate with location desirability. Going back to the 2013 Brookings Institution Report on patents per million residents, we can see that patent productivity is actually a Who's Who among America's hot spots. The top 20 includes San Jose, California; Boulder, Colorado; San Francisco, California; Austin, Texas; Seattle, Washington; Raleigh, North Carolina; San Diego, California; and Minneapolis, Minnesota. Disrespected Rochester, New York, is not held in such high esteem, hence the entire premise of this book.

Another angle of Rochester's ingenuity brings us back to the art scene. Although perhaps not validated statistically, the area seems to have an uncanny ability to recognize and foster talent, including acting talent. This most recent generation has been particularly fertile. Rochester has produced Taye Diggs, best known for his roles in *Rent*, "How Stella Got Her Groove Back," "Private Practice," and "The Best

Man." Another well-known local product is Kristen Wiig, whose resume includes "Saturday Night Live," "Bridesmaids," and "Despicable Me." Finally, perhaps the greatest pure actor of our generation, the late Philip Seymour Hoffman, was born and raised in the Rochester suburb of Fairport. Hoffman, who avoided the limelight, was the perfect embodiment of the metro area: no glitz, all substance.

The economic, scientific, and artistic creativity of Rochester is undeniable. While many have it pinned as a beat up Rust Belt town, the data would indicate otherwise.

11 Onward Thinking

The world is changing. In 1950, about 2.5 billion people inhabited the planet. Today, the world's population is over 7 billion. Between 2020 and 2030, that figure may rise to 8 billion. And by 2044, we could reach 9 billion. In America, the population has grown from 150 million in 1950 to about 316 million today. In 1960, Caucasians represented 85 percent of America. In 2011, that number was 63 percent. By 2050, it could be 47 percent.

Darwin's theory of evolution is barely 150 years old. One hundred years ago, women couldn't vote. The structure of DNA was published just over 60 years ago. Fifty years ago, segregation was rampant. Twenty years ago, most people had no idea about cell phones. Whether embraced or not, change occurs. Fortunately, over time, people come around. In Rochester, acceptance comes early and often.

In 1838, the great orator and writer Frederick Douglass escaped from slavery in Maryland. He ultimately settled in Rochester, where he began to publish the abolitionist newspaper *The North Star* and established Rochester as an important part of the Underground Railroad. He delivered his famous speech "What to the Slave is the Fourth of July," considered by some to be the greatest anti-slavery speech ever given. Douglass was once quoted as saying "I would unite with anybody to do right and with nobody to do wrong." He was apparently a man of his word, as one of his close friends in Rochester was the famous champion of women's voting rights, Susan B. Anthony. Anthony, born in Massachusetts, spent her adult life in Rochester, where she was once arrested for voting. (She never paid the fine.) Although she did not live to see it, the 19th amendment (which grants a woman's right to vote) is a living memorial of her work. Both Douglass and Anthony are buried in Rochester's Mount Hope Cemetery, and both are well-commemorated. Anthony's house is a popular museum, and Douglass inspired America's first monument to an African American.

Modern day Rochester, like many other metro areas in its region, suffers from the economic isolation of certain residents. Fortunately, it continues to fare rather well in terms of acceptance. When New York Governor Andrew Cuomo took office in 2011, he found it reasonable to eliminate discrimination by supporting same-sex marriage. While the measure passed relatively easily in the New York State Assembly, the New York State Senate had a Republican majority (as well as one Democrat against the bill.) This roadblock required at least 3 Republicans in the State Senate to cross the aisle. While standard wisdom would point to downstate New York, the downstate Republicans did not budge. Ultimately, four Republicans, all from upstate, gave their blessing. Senator James Alesi from Rochester was one of the four, choosing to support the bill despite knowing that this decision would end his political career as a Republican.

Recently, the United States Supreme Court ruled on the constitutionality of Christian prayer before town meetings. The case was brought before them due to the potential exclusionary nature of such prayer as well as the possible blending of Church and State. No matter one's opinion on the topic, the debate is clearly reasonable. Not surprisingly, the case originated in Greece, New York, a suburb of Rochester. Two women, one Jewish and one atheist, ultimately lost their quest but reminded us that Rochesterians are not always inclined to accept the status quo.

As our country and world change rapidly, we continue to learn from our prior mistakes. Rochester, both historically and currently, has embraced this process. Many would agree that such a quality is a good one and one that bodes well for the future.

Afterword

America, as one of the world's largest and most populous countries, offers innumerable living options. While a dream job can make such a choice rather easy, most of us are left with a decision to make. Typically, as was the case with the baseball and soccer industries, the eye test and popular perception have played a large role in such decisions. Being perfectly honest, Rochester, New York, has not fared well by such "measures." With the move toward data-driven decision-making, unexpected findings have become the norm. Such data-driven analysis of 11 metropolitan-defining qualities has not let us down: podunk Rochester, New York, is actually a phenomenal place to live. Other metro areas clearly outperform Rochester in some of the 11 measures. That said, Rochester's consistent performance over all 11 measures is difficult to replicate. For example, the New York City area will clearly shine in music/art and leisure. Unfortunately, cost of living and commute times are far from optimal. Similarly, one could imagine a smaller metro area with a very low cost of living that comes at the expense of top-level education, music/art, and ingenuity. Finally, one might find a region that matches Rochester reasonably well. A closer look, however, could show less acceptance of change.

Even two of Rochester's perceived weaknesses come with intertwined strengths. High taxes contribute to superlative public education and near universal health care. Snowy winters bring mild summers and repel natural disasters.

As it stands, Rochester, New York, is a remarkably balanced place. It is vibrant yet peaceful, intelligent yet modest, and enriching yet affordable. I am delighted to now call it home. I encourage others to do the same.

List of Relevant References
(listed once in order of appearance)

Introduction

US Census Bureau. American Fact Finder. Available at http://factfinder2.census.gov/faces/nav/jsf/pages/index.xhtml. Accessed October 26, 2014.

1. Economy

Applebome, Peter. Despite Long Slide by Kodak, Company Town Avoids Decay. *The New York Times:* January 16, 2012. Available at http://www.nytimes.com/2012/01/17/nyregion/despite-long-slide-by-kodak-rochester-avoids-decay.html?pagewanted=all&_r=0. Accessed May 28, 2014.

Downtown Market Report. Rochester Downtown Development Corporation. Available at http://www.rochesterdowntown.com/wp_rddc/wp-content/uploads/2014/05/MARKET-REPORT-Publisher-Version-April-2014.pdf. Accessed June 14, 2014.

Berube, Alan. Global Metromonitor. Available at http://www.brookings.edu/research/interactives/global-metro-monitor. Accessed June 16, 2014.

LaCara, Len. Rochester Jobless Rate Lowest in 6 Years. *Democrat and Chronicle*: May 20, 2014.

Available at http://www.democratandchronicle.com/story/money/business/2014/05/20/rochester-jobless-rate-lowest-years/9328315/. Accessed May 28, 2014.

NY unemployment falls to five-plus year low. *Democrat and Chronicle*: May 15, 2014. Available at http://www.democratandchronicle.com/story/money/business/2014/05/15/rochester-job-creation-numbers/9136671/. Accessed May 28, 2014.

Best Companies 2014. *Fortune*. Available at http://fortune.com/best-companies/google-1/. Accessed June 28, 2014.

Upadhye, Neeti. Wegmans tops supermarket survey; Wal-Mart ranks last. *Democrat and Chronicle*: March 27, 2014. Available at http://www.usatoday.com/story/news/nation-now/2014/03/27/grocery-stores-consumer-reports-rankings/6967537/. Accessed June 28, 2014.

Best Small & Medium Workplaces 2014. *Fortune*. Available at http://www.greatplacetowork.com/best-companies/best-small-a-medium-workplaces. Accessed June 28, 2014.

Greater Rochester Enterprise. Labor. (Data from U.S. Department of Education, 2013.) Available at http://www.rochesterbiz.com/DoingBusinessHere/BusinessInformation/Labor.aspx. Accessed June 28, 2014.

2. Education

Spector, Joseph. Once again, NY spends most in US on schools. *Democrat and Chronicle*: May 23, 2014. Available at http://www.democratand chronicle.com/story/news/politics/blogs/vote-up/2014/ 05/23/once-again-ny-spends-most-in-u-s-on-schools/9497147/. Accessed June 20, 2014.

Zillow. Home Values. Available at http://www.zillow.com/home-values/. Accessed October 27, 2014.

Best Colleges Rankings. *US News & World Report*. Available at http://colleges.usnews.rankingsand reviews.com/best-colleges. Accessed June 21, 2014.

The Top 50 NIH-Funded Universities. *Genetic Engineering & Biotechnology News*: August 19, 2013. Available at http://www.genengnews.com/insight-and-intelligence/the-top-50-nih-funded-universi-ties/77899877/?page=1. Accessed June 21, 2014.

2013 Top 30 Music School Ranking in US. US College Rankings. Available at http://www.us collegeranking.org/music/2013-top-30-music-school-ranking-in-u-s.html#axzz33zNdChlP. Accessed June 22, 2014.

10 College Business Incubators We're Most Excited About. Available at http://www.best collegesonline.com/blog/2012/07/30/10-college-

business-incubators-were-most-excited-about/. Accessed June 22, 2014.

Sperling's Best Places. Most Competitive Colleges. Available at http://www.bestplaces.net/docs /studies/competitivecolleges.aspx. Accessed June 23, 2014.

Snider, Susannah. Best Values in Public Colleges, 2013. *Kiplinger's Personal Finance*: Februrary 2013. Available at http://www.kiplinger.com/article/ college/T014-C000-S002-best-values-in-public-colleges-2013.html. Accessed June 23, 2014.

College Guide: Rankings – 2010 Community Colleges. *Washington Monthly*. Available at http:// www.washingtonmonthly.com/college_guide/ rankings_2010/community_colleges.php. Accessed June 24, 2014.

Greater Rochester Enterprise. Education. (Data from American Community Survey 1-year estimates, 2012.) Available at http://www.rochester biz.com/LivingHere/Education.aspx. Accessed June 25, 2014.

Cities with the Most College-Educated Residents. *The New York Times*: May 30, 2012. Available at http://www.nytimes.com/interactive/2012/05/31/ us/education-in-metro-areas.html?_r=0. Accessed June 27, 2014.

America's Smartest Cities. *The Daily Beast*: November 3, 2010. Available at http://www.the dailybeast.com/articles/2010/11/03/americas-smartest-cities.html. Accessed June 20, 2014.

O, Tina. Study: Smartest Cities. *CreditDonkey*: March 10, 2014. Available at http://www.credit donkey.com/where-smartest.html. Accessed June 20, 2014.

Florida, Richard. Are These America's Brainiest Cities? *The Atlantic* City Lab: June 25, 2013. Available at http://www.citylab.com/housing/2013/06/are-these-americas-brainiest-cities/5941/. Accessed June 21, 2014.

3. Music/Art

Xerox Rochester International Jazz Festival. Available at http://www.rochesterjazz.com/php/about.php. Accessed June 28, 2014.

The House of Guitars. Available at http://www.houseofguitars.com/Press-Room.html. Accessed October 30, 2014.

Florida, Richard. The Geography of America's Music Scenes. *The Atlantic* City Lab: August 6, 2012. Available at http://www.citylab.com/design/2012/08/geography-americas-music-scenes/2709/. Accessed July 22, 2014.

Memorial Art Gallery Fact Sheet. Available at
http://mag.rochester.edu/pr/News/mag_factsheet
14.pdf. Accessed October 31, 2014.

Corn Hill Arts Festival. Available at http://
cornhillartsfestival.com/. Accessed July 23, 2014.

George Eastman House International Museum of
Photography and Film. Available at http://www.
eastmanhouse.org/museum/ataglance.php.
Accessed July 23, 2014.

Loudon, Bennett J. Leading role at Geva Theatre.
Democrat and Chronicle: May 28, 2013. Available at
http://whatsuproc.com/art/story/113783.
Accessed July 24, 2014.

Nazareth College – The Basics. *The Princeton
Review*. Available at http://www.princetonreview.
com/NazarethCollegeofRochester.aspx. Accessed
November 2, 2014.

Clapp, Jake. Rochester Fringe attendance hits new
high. *City Newspaper*: October 3, 2014. Available at
http://www.rochestercitynewspaper.com/rochester/
rochester-fringe-festival-attendance-hits-new/
Content?oid=2442559. Accessed November 4,
2014.

Roberts, Cathy. Smithsonian honoring Wendell
Castle, Albert Paley. *Democrat and Chronicle*: February 18, 2014. Available at http://www.democrat

andchronicle.com/story/staff/2014/02/18/albert-paley-wendell-castle-smithsonian-craft-show/5584937/. Accessed July 25, 2014.

2011 Creative Industries – 100 Most Populated US Cities. Americans for the Arts. Data Source: Dun & Bradstreet, January 2011. Available at http://www.sandiego.gov/arts-culture/pdf/news/2012/popcities11.pdf. Accessed July 25, 2014.

4. Leisure

Finger Lakes Wine. Available at http://www.fingerlakes.com/wine. Accessed August 1, 2014.

Krigbaum, Megan. World's Best Riesling Wine Regions. *Food & Wine*. Available at http://www.foodandwine.com/articles/worlds-best-riesling-wine-regions. Accessed August 1, 2014.

Fox Run Vineyards Awards. Available at http://www.foxrunvineyards.com/NEW%20Winery-Awards.asp. Accessed August 1, 2014.

Polland, Jennifer and Zeveloff, Julie. 50 Trips You Need To Take In The United States. *Business Insider*: March 11, 2013. Available at http://www.businessinsider.com/50-trips-to-take-in-the-united-states-2013-3?op=1. Accessed August 1, 2014.

Wegmans Company Overview. Available at https://www.wegmans.com/webapp/wcs/stores/ser

vlet/CategoryDisplay?storeId=10052&identifier=
CATEGORY_2441. Accessed August 2, 2014.

Novak, Jess. America's 50 Best Coffee Shops. *The Daily Meal*: June 6, 2014. Available at http://www.thedailymeal.com/america-s-50-best-coffee-shops/41514. Accessed August 3, 2014.

Lankes, Tiffany. A day at the Rochester Public Market: 300 vendors, 25,000 customers. *Democrat & Chronicle*: July 27, 2012. Available at http://roc.democratandchronicle.com/article/20120727/FLAVORS/307270022/A-day-Rochester-Public-Market-300-vendors-25-000-customers. Accessed August 3, 2014.

America's Favorite Farmers Markets. American Farmland Trust. Available at http://action.farmland.org/site/PageServer?pagename=winners2010. Accessed August 4, 2014.

Greater Rochester Enterprise. Rochester Rankings. Available at http://www.rochesterbiz.com/DoingBusinessHere/BusinessInformation/RochesterRankings.aspx. Accessed August 4, 2014.

Visit Rochester. Available at http://www.visitrochester.com/index.cfm. Accessed August 4, 2014.

Letchworth State Park. New York State Office of Parks, Recreation & Historic Preservation. Available at http://nysparks.com/parks/79/details.aspx. Accessed August 5, 2014.

The 10 Best Golf Cities in America. Available at http://www.golf.com/photos/10-best-golf-cities-america/golf-cities-rochester-ny. Accessed August 5, 2014.

Whitten, Ron. 2013-14 Ranking: America's 100 Greatest Golf Courses. *Golf Digest*: February 2013. Available at http://www.golfdigest.com/golf-courses/2013-02/americas-100-greatest-golfcourses-ranking. Accessed August 5, 2014.

Bristol Mountain Winter Resort. Available at https://www.bristolmountain.com/. Accessed November 10, 2014.

Resort Guide 2013-14. Posted September 18, 2013. Available at http://www.skinet.com/ski/2014 resortguide. Accessed August 6, 2014.

Roth, Leo. Rochester struts its stuff at London Olympics. August 12, 2012. Available in *Democrat and Chronicle* paid archive or at http:// mvrocket.com/2012/08/12/rochester-new-york-leads-country-in-olympic-athletes/. Accessed August 7, 2014.

Olmsted, Larry. 12 Best Children's Museums In The US. *Forbes*: January 30, 2012. Available at http://www.forbes.com/sites/larryolmsted/2012/01/30/12-best-childrens-museums-in-the-u-s/. Accessed August 8, 2014.

Sangiorgio, Maureen P. The 10 Best Children's Museums. Available at http://www.parents.com/

fun/vacation/us-destinations/the-10-best-childrens-museums/. Accessed August 8, 2014.

World's Oldest Operating Amusement Parks. National Amusement Park Historical Association. Available at http://www.napha.org/LIBRARY/FactsFigures/WorldsOldestOperatingAmusement Parks/tabid/70/Default.aspx. Accessed August 9, 2014.

Levy, Francesca. America's Best Places To Raise A Family. *Forbes*: June 7, 2010. Available at http://www.forbes.com/2010/06/04/best-places-family-lifestyle-real-estate-cities-kids.html. Accessed August 10, 2014.

Best Cities for Families. *Kiplinger*: July 2012. Available at http://www.kiplinger.com/slideshow/real-estate/T006-S001-best-cities-for-families/index.html. Accessed August 10, 2014.

2013 Minor League Markets: The rankings. *Street & Smith's Sports Business Journal*: August 12, 2013. Available at http://www.sportsbusinessdaily.com/Journal/Issues/2013/08/12/Research-and-Ratings/Top-minor-league-markets.aspx. Accessed August 10, 2014.

5. Cost of Living

Pyykkonen, Antti-Jussi et al. Stressful Life Events and the Metabolic Syndrome. *Diabetes Care* 33:

378-384, 2010. Available at http://care.diabetes journals.org/content/33/2/378.full.pdf. Accessed June 1, 2014.

Greenhouse, Steven. Our Economic Pickle. *The New York Times*: January 12, 2013. Available at http://www.nytimes.com/2013/01/13/sunday-review/americas-productivity-climbs-but-wages-stagnate.html?_r=0. Accessed June 1, 2014.

Vardi, Nathan and Whelan, David. The Best Places To Buy A Home Right Now. *Forbes*: May 9, 2011. Available at http://www.forbes.com/2011/05/09/best-places-to-buy-a-home-now.html. Accessed June 1, 2014.

Levy, Francesca. America's Most Affordable Cities. *Forbes*: October 28, 2010. Available at http://www.forbes.com/2010/10/28/affordable-cities-cost-of-living-lifestyle-real-estate-salaries.html. Accessed June 2, 2014.

10th Annual Demographia International Housing Affordability Survey: 2014. Available at http://www.demographia.com/dhi.pdf. Accessed June 2, 2014.

City of Rochester News Release – Rochester Takes No. 1 in MSN Real Estate 'Most Livable Bargain Markets.' Available at http://www.cityofrochester.gov/article.aspx?id=8589948906. Accessed November 3, 2014.

Rich, Spencer. Rochester, NY, Shapes Revolution in Near-Universal Health Care Plan. From *The Washinton Post*. Published in *Los Angeles Times*: November 29, 1992. Available at http://articles.latimes.com/1992-11-29/news/mn-2738_1_blue-cross. Accessed June 3, 2014.

Variation in Healthcare Spending. Institute of Medicine. Available at http://iom.edu/~/media/Files/Report%20Files/2013/Geographic-Variation2/geovariation_slides.pdf. Accessed November 3, 2014.

Gardner, Kent. Rochester has lowest monthly premiums in ACA's exchange. *Rochester Business Journal*: August 16, 2013. Available at http://www.rbj.net/article.asp?aID=197784. Accessed June 3, 2014.

Why choose Rochester, NY? Greater Rochester Enterprise. Available at http://www.rochesterbiz.com/Portals/0/PortalFiles/Documents/Affordable healthcarebrochureFinal.pdf. Accessed June 3, 2014.

6. Commute Times

Hoehner, Christine et al. Commuting Distance, Cardiorespiratory Fitness, and Metabolic Risk. *American Journal of Preventive Medicine*, Volume 42, Issue 6: June 2012. Available at http://

www.ajpmonline.org/article/S07493797(12)00167
-5/abstract. Accessed May 29, 2014.

Lowrey, Annie. Your Commute Is Killing You. *Slate*:May 26, 2011. Available at http://www.slate. com/articles/business/moneybox/2011/05/your_c ommute_is_killing_you.1.html. Accessed May 29, 2014.

Sandow, Erika. Til Work Do Us Part: The Social Fallacy of Long-distance Commuting. *Urban Studies*: Published online August 7, 2013. Available at http://usj.sagepub.com/content/early/2013 /08/06/0042098013498280. Accessed May 31, 2014.

10 Best Cities For Commuters. *Kiplinger*: February 2011. Available at http://www.kiplinger.com/ slideshow/real-estate/T006-S001-10-best-cities- for-commuters-slide-show/index.html. Accessed June 2, 2014.

Hrywna, Mark. Volunteering Continues Upward Trend In Hours, Value. *The NonProfit Times*: February 24, 2014. Available at http://www.the nonprofittimes.com/news-articles/volunteering- continues-upward-trend-in-hours-value-2/. Accessed October 27, 2014.

10 Least Stressed Out Cities. CNN Money. Available at http://money.cnn.com/gallery/pf/ 2014/06

/25/least-stressed-out-cities/2.html. Accessed August 31, 2014.

7. Weather

Erdman, Jon. America's 20 Snowiest Major Cities. April 5, 2014. Available at http://www.weather.com/news/weather-winter/20-snowiest-large-cities-america-20140130?pageno=1. Accessed May 27, 2014.

Rochester NY Snowfall Totals & Accumulation Averages. Current Results. Available at http://www.currentresults.com/Weather/New-York/Places/rochester-snowfall-totals-snow-accumulation-averages.php. Accessed May 27, 2014.

Erdman, Jon. America's 20 Coldest Major Cities. January 27, 2014. Available at http://www.weather.com/news/weather-winter/20-coldest-large-cities-america-20140107. Accessed May 27, 2014.

Erdman, Jon. America's Safest Weather Cities. August 10, 2012. Available at http://www.weather.com/news/safest-weather-cities-20120808?pageno=1. Accessed May 27, 2014.

McDermott, Meaghan M. Watchdog report: How dangerous is driving? *Democrat and Chronicle*: March 2, 2014. Available at http://www.democratandchronicle.com/story/news/2014/

03/02/rochester-roads-accidents-driving-dangers/
5929951/. Accessed May 27, 2014.

Osborn, Liz. Coolest US Cities in Summer. Current Results. Available at http://www.current results.com/Weather-Extremes/US/coldest-cities-summer.php. Accessed May 27, 2014.

8. Taxes

Tax Foundation, Facts & Figures. Available at http://taxfoundation.org/sites/taxfoundation.org/f iles/docs/ff2013.pdf. Accessed June 21, 2014

Moreno, Tonya. Highest and Lowest Property Taxes by County. Available at http://taxes. about.com/od/statetaxes/a/Property-taxes-high-est-lowest.htm. Accessed June 21, 2014.

Best High Schools Rankings 2014. *US News & World Report.* Available at http://www.usnews. com/education/best-high-schools/national-rank-ings. Accessed June 22, 2014.

Total Medicaid Spending, 2012. The Henry J. Kaiser Family Foundation. Available at http:// kff.org/medicaid/state-indicator/total-medicaid-spending/. Accessed June 22, 2014.

Health Insurance Coverage of the Total Population, 2013. The Henry J. Kaiser Family Foundation. Available at http://kff.org/other/state-indicator/total-population/. Accessed October 27, 2014.

25 Best and Worst Health-Care Cities. *The Daily Beast*: January 18, 2011. Available at http://www. thedailybeast.com/articles/2011/01/18/health-care-reform-the-25-most-and-least-insured-cities. html. Accessed June 22, 2014.

9. Transportation

List of US cities with high transit ridership. Wikipedia. Available at http://en.wikipedia.org/ wiki/List_of_U.S._cities_with_high_transit_riders hip. Accessed June 10, 2014.

New transit center only part of improvements by RGRTA. *Democrat and Chronicle*: March 12, 2014. Available at http://www.democratandchronicle. com/story/opinion/editorials/2014/03/12/new-transit-center-part-improvements-rgrta/6304213/. Accessed June 10, 2014.

America's Best Bike Cities. *Bicycling Magazine*. Available at http://www.bicycling.com/news/ featured-stories/bicyclings-top-50. Accessed June 11, 2014.

Philly is One of the Nation's Most Walkable Cities. *The Philadelphia News*: November 12, 2011. Available at http://thephilanews.com/walking-best-places-3735.htm. Accessed June 14, 2014.

McKenzie, Brian. Modes Less Traveled - Bicycling and Walking to Work in the United States: 2008-2012. May 2014. Available at http://www.census.gov/prod/2014pubs/acs-25.pdf. Accessed June 14, 2014.

The ROC Experience. The Greater Rochester International Airport 2013 Annual Report. Available at http://www2.monroecounty.gov/files/air port/docs/2013%20ROC%20Annual%20Report %20Final.pdf. Accessed June 15, 2014.

10. Ingenuity

Rothwell, Jonathan, et al. Patenting Prosperity: Invention and Economic Performance in the United States and its Metropolitan Areas. Available at http://www.brookings.edu/~/media/Re search/Files/Reports/2013/02/patenting%20pros perity%20rothwell/patenting%20prosperity%20r othwell.pdf. Accessed July 11, 2014.

Greenberg, Andy. In Depth: America's Most Innovative Cities. *Forbes*: May 24, 2010. Available at http://www.forbes.com/2010/05/24/patents-funding-jobs-technology-innovative-cities_slide.html. Accessed July 12, 2014.

Zhang, Qian et al. Characterizing scientific production and consumption in Physics. *Scientific Reports* 3, Article No. 1640: April 10, 2013. Available at http://www.nature.com/srep/2013/130410/

srep01640/full/srep01640.html. Accessed July 14,
2014.

11. Onward Thinking

U.S. Census Bureau, International Data Base, June
2011 Update. Available at http://www.census.gov/
population/international/data/idb/worldpopgraph.
php. Accessed May 29, 2014.

Wade, Lisa. U.S. Racial/Ethnic Demographics:
1960, Today, and 2050. *The Society Pages*: November 14, 2012. Available at http://thesociety
pages.org/socimages/2012/11/14/u-s-racialethnic-
demographics-1960-today-and-2050/. Accessed
May 29, 2014.

Index

Y

Z

CPSIA information can be obtained at www.ICGtesting.com
Printed in the USA
BVOW02s1939030116

431635BV00001B/47/P

9 781457 535178